Carpenters Joke Book

The Ultimate Collection of Carpenter Jokes

Published by Glowworm Press
7 Nuffield Way
Abingdon OX14 1RL
By Chester Croker

Jokes for Carpenters

These jokes for carpenters will make you giggle. You will find some classic old carpenter jokes that we have pulled out of the woodwork and also plenty of new carpenter jokes which will make you laugh out loud.

We hope you enjoy our collection of the very best carpenter jokes and puns which are guaranteed to get you laughing.

FOREWORD

When I was asked to write a foreword to this book I felt elated.

That is until I was told that I was the last resort by the author, Chester Croker, and that everyone else he had approached had said they couldn't do it!

I have known Chester for a number of years and his ability to create jokes is absolutely incredible. He is an expert at crafting clever puns and amusing gags and I feel he is the ideal man to put together a joke book about our profession – he is simply a cut above others.

He will be glad you have bought this book, as he has an expensive lifestyle to maintain.

Even Edges

Table of Contents

Chapter 1: Carpenter Jokes

If you're looking for funny carpenter jokes you've certainly come to the right place.

Here you will find some old carpenter jokes, some re-worked funny stories and also some new gags, and we really hope that you enjoy our collection of some of the very best carpenter jokes and puns around.

We've got some great one-liners to start with, plenty of quick fire questions and answers themed gags, some story led jokes and as a bonus some cheesy pick-up lines for carpenters.

This mixture of carpenter jokes will prove that carpenters have a good sense of humor.

Chapter 2: One Liner Carpenter Jokes

The experienced carpenter really nailed it, but the new guy screwed everything up.

A mother told her carpenter son "Well, if women don't find you handsome, they will at least find you handy."

Did you hear about the drunk guy that was attacked by a carpenter? I heard he was hammered.

Did you hear about the two lesbian carpenters that built a house? There was not a stud in the place. It was all tongue in groove.

Did you hear about the cross-eyed carpenter?

He couldn't see eye to eye with his customers.

Wood you consider lumberjacks to be yew man beings? It's a difficult question, but I have to axe.

A carpenter's wife asked her husband to pass her lipstick yesterday but he passed her a super-glue stick instead by mistake. She still isn't talking to him.

Yo mama so old the carpenter uses her crotch as sandpaper.

Did you hear about the work-shy carpenter who ran out of sick days so he called in dead.

I saw an argument between a carpenter and a hairdresser today. They were going at it hammer and tongs.

A team of carpenters have been at my neighbor's house for a few weeks. The rumor is they're building a library, but it's all been a bit hush-hush.

I'd like to build a barn over Christmas, if I can find space in my shed-yule.

Did you hear about the trainee carpenter who stole a calendar? He got twelve months.

I got called pretty yesterday and it felt good. Actually, the full sentence was "You're a pretty bad carpenter." but I'm choosing to focus on the positive.

My carpenter friend got educated at a boarding school.

Jesus once said "He who lives by the sword, will die by the sword." He was a carpenter that died by being nailed to a piece of wood, so he might have had a point.

A carpenter friend of mine gave me some great advice, saying I should put something away for a rainy day. I've gone for an umbrella.

The first carpenter screwed up the job, but the second one really nailed it.

A chippie wanted to buy something for his miserable boss, so he bought him a new chair. His boss won't let him plug it in though.

Carpenters enjoy showering.

They work up a good lather.

Chapter 3: Q&A Carpenter Jokes

Q: Why did the guitarist get fired as a carpenter?

A: He was shredding the floor.

Q: Why did the carpenter join the army?

A: Because he wanted to be a Drill Sergeant.

Q: What does a carpenter do after a one night stand?

A: The second nightstand.

Q: Why is it easy to get Christmas gifts for carpenters?

A: All they want for Christmas is yew.

Q: How did the carpenter do on his interview?

A: He nailed it.

Q: What did the foreman say to the carpenter who was shirking his work?

A: Quit plane around.

Q: What did the carpenter say when asked if his sandpaper was rough enough?

A: Of coarse it is.

Q: How did the carpenter cut wood in half, just by looking at it?

A: He just saw it with his own eyes.

Q: What did the car-painter say to the carpenter?
A: You sound just like me.

Q: What's the difference between Jesus and other carpenters?

A: Jesus may actually return some day.

Q: How does a carpenter effectively build stairs?

A: He thinks one step ahead.

Q: Why do carpenters have such large toolboxes?

A: Because they have to be awl-encompassing.

Q: What happened when a carpenter crossed a chili pepper, a shovel and a terrier?

A: He got a hot-diggity-dog.

Q: Who was the first carpenter?

A: Eve - She made Adam's banana stand.

Q: What do you call a carpenter who is happy every Monday?

A: Retired.

Q: Why is the tasty MILF in the house next door a carpenter's dream?

A: She is as flat as a board and easy to nail.

Q: What do carpenters and cam-girls have in common?

A: They both bang their fingers for a living.

Q: What's a carpenter's prototype of a bar seat called?

A: A stool sample.

Q: Why do some carpenters get slapped by women?

A: Because they want to show women their caulk.

Q: What do you call a Middle Eastern carpenter?

A: Ahmed Ashed.

Q: What happens when a carpenter drinks with his wife?

A: He gets hammered and she gets nailed.

Q: Why did the carpenter's wife leave him?

A: He was screwing around when he was supposed to be nailing her.

Q: Did you hear the miracle about the blind carpenter?

A: He picked up his hammer and saw.

Q: What happened to the door after the carpenter told him he was being replaced?

A: It got angry and became unhinged.

Q: Why does President Trump need a good carpenter?

A: To fix his cabinet.

Q: What does a carpenter do after a one night stand?

A: A matching one for the other side of the bed.

Q: Why did the cannibal carpenter get disciplined by his boss?

A: For buttering up his clients.

Q: Which nails do carpenters hate hitting?

A: Their finger nails.

Chapter 4: Short Carpenter Jokes

A carpenter is struggling to find a parking space at the builder's yard.

"Lord," he prayed. "I can't stand this. If you find me a space, I swear I'll give up the booze and will go to church every Sunday."

Suddenly, the clouds part and the sun shines down onto an empty parking spot.

Without hesitation, the carpenter says: "Never mind Lord, I found one."

A carpenter was giving evidence about an accident he had witnessed. The lawyer for the defendant was trying to discredit him and asked him how far away he was from the accident.

The carpenter replied, "Twenty-eight feet, six and one-half inches."

"What? How come you can be so sure of that distance?" asked the lawyer.

"Well, I knew sooner or later some idiot would ask me. So I measured it!" replied the carpenter.

A carpenter called Paddy calls up his local paper and asks "How much would it be to put an ad in your paper?"

"Four dollars an inch," a woman replies. "Why? What are you selling?"

"A ten-foot ladder," said Paddy before slamming the phone down.

Two carpenters are talking about sex.

The first carpenter says he thinks sex is 80% work and 20% pleasure while the second carpenter says that sex is 20% work and 80% pleasure. They decide to ask their apprentice what he thinks.

"Sex is 100% all pleasure" says the apprentice.

"Why do you say that?" ask the carpenters.

The apprentice replies "Well, if there is any work involved, you two get me to do it."

A carpenter goes to the doctor with a hearing problem.

The doctor says, "Can you describe the symptoms to me?"

The carpenter replies "Yes. Homer is a fat yellow lazy man and his wife Marge is skinny with big blue hair."

A carpenter in my area went to jail for dealing drugs.

I've been one of his customers for over five years, and I had no clue he was a carpenter.

A retired carpenter was walking along the road one day when he came across a frog.

He reached down, picked the frog up, and started to put it in his pocket.

As he did so, the frog said in a croaky voice, "Kiss me on the lips and I'll turn into a beautiful woman and show you a really good time."

The old carpenter continued to put the frog into his pocket.

The frog croaked, "Didn't you hear what I said?"

The carpenter looked down at the frog and said, "Yes, I did, but at my age I think I'd rather have a talking frog."

A carpenter tries to enter a smart cocktail bar wearing a shirt open at the collar, and he is met by a bouncer who tells him that he needs to wear a necktie to gain admission.

So the carpenter goes to his car to try and find a necktie but he can't find one.

However he knows he has some jump leads in his boot; and in desperation he ties these around his neck, and somehow creates a reasonable looking knot with the ends of the cables dangling down.

He goes back to the bar where the bouncer gives him the once over, and says: "You can come in now – but just don't start anything!"

A dog walks into a pub, and says to the barman, "Can I have a pint of lager and a packet of crisps please."

The barman is amazed by the talking dog and says to him, "You are amazing – you should join the circus."

The talking dog replies, "Why? Do they need carpenters?"

A guy goes into his local lumber yard, and asks for some 2 x 4s.

The salesman asks "How long do you want them?" to which the guy replies "Oh, quite a while, I'm going to build a garage with them."

The homeowner was delighted with the quality of work the carpenter had done on his house.

"You did a great job." he said and he paid the chippie.

"Also, in order to thank-you, here's an extra $100 for you to take the missus out to dinner."

Later that night, the doorbell rang and it was the carpenter.

The homeowner asked him, "What's the matter, did you forget something?"

"Nope." replied the carpenter, "I'm just here to take your missus out to dinner like you asked."

A team of carpenters were building a wooden patio outside my house.

I had just finished washing the hall floor when one of the carpenters asked to come inside and use the toilet.

With dismay I looked at his muddy boots and my newly polished floor.

"Just a minute," I said, "I'll put down some newspaper."

"That's all right, madam" he responded. "I'm house trained."

A carpenter meets up with his blonde girlfriend as she's picking up her car from the mechanic.

"Everything ok with your car now?" he asks.

"Yes, thank goodness," the dipsy blonde replies.

"Weren't you worried the mechanic might try to rip you off?"

"Yes, but he didn't. I was so relieved when he told me that all I needed was blinker fluid!"

A carpenter took his cross-eyed dog to the vet.

The vet picked the dog up to examine him and said, "Sorry, I'm going to have to put him down."

The carpenter said "Oh no! It's not that bad is it?"

The vet replied, "No, he's just very heavy."

A doctor hired a carpenter to do some work around his house.

During the job, the doctor looked over the chippie's shoulder as he was applying a piece of molding to cover his uneven cut.

The doctor said "That's an easy way to hide your mistakes."

The carpenter replied "Yes, I don't need six feet of soil to hide my mistakes."

A carpenter called Mick and a roofer called Gary were working on a building site.

Gary is up on the scaffolding on the first floor and accidentally cuts off his ear, and he yelled down to Mick "Hey, look out for my ear I just cut off."

Mick looks around and calls up to Gary, "Is this your ear?"

Gary looks down and says "Nah. Mine had a pencil behind it!"

A young carpenter is sitting at a bar after work one night, when a burly sweaty construction worker sits down next to him.

They start talking and after a little while the conversation eventually gets on to nuclear war.

The carpenter asks the construction worker, "What you would do if you were to hear the sirens go off, and know that you've just got twenty minutes left to live?"

The construction worker replies, "Well. that's easy – I am going to make it with anything that moves."

The construction worker then asks the chippie what he would do to which he gently replies, "I am going to try and keep perfectly still."

A carpenter complained to an old friend of his that his wife didn't satisfy him anymore.

His buddy advised that he find another woman on the side, and pretty sharpish too.

When they met up a month later, the chippie told his friend "I took your advice. I managed to find a woman on the side, yet my wife still doesn't satisfy me!"

Chapter 5: Longer Carpenter Jokes

Three Friends

Ron is chatting to his pals, Jim and Shamus.

Jim says, "I think my wife is having an affair with a carpenter. The other day I came home and found a saw under our bed and it wasn't mine."

Shamus then confides, "Well I think my wife is having an affair with an electrician. The other day I found wire cutters under the bed and they weren't mine."

Ron thinks for a minute and then says, "Well I think my wife is having an affair with a horse."

Both Jim and Shamus look at him in disbelief.

Ron sees them looking at him and says, "No, seriously. The other day I came home early and found a jockey under our bed."

Train Passengers

A carpenter, a plasterer, a beautiful lady, and an old woman were on a train, sitting 2x2 facing each other.

The train went into a tunnel and when the carriage went completely dark, a loud smack was heard. When the train came out of the tunnel back into the light the plasterer had a red hand print on his face where he had been slapped.

The old lady thought, "That plasterer must have groped the young lady in the dark and she slapped him."

The hottie thought, "That plasterer must have tried to grope me, got the old lady by mistake, and she slapped him."

The plasterer thought, "That carpenter must have groped the hottie, she thought it was me, and slapped me."

The carpenter sat there thinking, "I can't wait for another tunnel so I can slap that plasterer again!"

Master Van Echo

There once was a man named Poly Van Echo who worked as a carpenter in the Middle Ages. He spent years honing his craft, working under many master builders until one day he rose to prominence and became the official carpenter to the King.

The King came to him during a particularly rainy season, and said, "Master Van Echo, the rain has caused all the bridges in our kingdom to rot. Citizens are unable to go to market, farmers cannot bring their crops forth to sell, under risk of a collapse. Can you do something?"

Poly went to work immediately rebuilding the bridges, it took many weeks, but finally all the wood work in the kingdom was rebuilt, stronger than ever.

He came to the palace and said, "My liege, the work is complete."

The King replied, "Yes, the bridges are rebuilt, but what if the rains were to come again? Will they not give way to rot again?"

The carpenter shook his head, "No your highness, for I have developed a special compound that promises to keep our bridges free of rot, see how they glimmer in the sun with renewed strength against the rain."

The King nodded his approval and called his closest advisers to conference, after a few moments he spoke "Master Van Echo, for your service to the kingdom, we grant you land and title."

"Yes Poly, you're a Thane."

A Genie In The Lamp

A carpenter finds a genie in a lamp, and the genie tells him "I can only grant you one wish. What is it that you would like?"

The carpenter responds, "Carpentry is my passion. I would love to be able to talk to my tools. They are my friends, after all."

The genie makes it so.

Later, the carpenter is working on the frame of a house when he sees his hammer next to him. The carpenter says to the hammer, "Well, I can talk to my tools now. What would you like to say?"

The hammer replies, "I'm hammer."

"Yes, I know that" says the carpenter. "Is that it?"

"I'm hammer," says the hammer.

The carpenter is frustrated and turns to his trusty wrench. The carpenter says, "What about you? What can you say?"

"I'm wrench," says the wrench.

Now the carpenter is really frustrated. He asks his saw, ladder, tape measure, and screw driver the same questions, only to hear, "I'm saw, I'm ladder, I'm tape measure, I'm screw driver and so on."

The carpenter gives up for the day. He drives home, knowing that he may be able to forget his wish and relax in front of the television. He gets home and sees a plank next to the sofa.

"What is going on?" exclaims the carpenter. To which he gets the reply "I'm bored."

The Golfers

A carpenter was playing a round of golf with his priest and the carpenter was playing baldy.

On the third hole he swung his club and missed the ball. He yelled "God damn it – I missed."

The priest rebuked him "You shouldn't curse, or God might punish you."

The carpenter waved him off, swung again, missed the ball again and once again he shouted out "God damn it – I missed."

The priest exclaims "The Lord might strike you down with lightning for taking his name in vain."

The carpenter laughed him off, swung a third time, missed the ball again, and again the carpenter yelled out "God damn it – I missed."

Before the priest could say anything, an ominous dark cloud suddenly gathered out of the blue sky and a vicious lightning bolt came down and hit the priest, killing him instantly.

A thunderous voice deep voice was then heard from above saying "God damn it – I missed."

The Pearly Gates

A carpenter dies in a fishing accident on his 40th birthday and finds himself greeted at the Pearly Gates by a brass band. Saint Peter runs over, shakes his hand and says "Congratulations!"

"Congratulations for what?" asks the carpenter.

"We are celebrating the fact that you lived to be 100 years old." says Saint Peter.

"But that's not true," says the carpenter. "I only lived to be forty."

"That's impossible," says Saint Peter, "we added up your time sheets on your invoices."

The Parrot and the Carpenter

A carpenter is called to the house of a cute little old lady. There is a restless Doberman sitting in the kitchen drooling and growling under his breath, and a parrot whistling contentedly next to him on his perch.

Half-way through the job, the little old lady tells him she's going to the grocery store. The carpenter asks the little old lady if he'll be safe while she's away to which she smiles and says, "Oh yes! Poopsie is so sweet. He wouldn't hurt a fly. He's a good doggie."

Then the old lady adds, "Oh. But whatever you do, do NOT say anything to the parrot."

Relieved, the carpenter resumes his work. After the little old lady leaves, the parrot starts making a horrible racket and is calling the carpenter all manner of rude names.

Losing his temper, the carpenter glares at the bird and screams, "Shut up, you feathered fruitcake!" and he goes back to his work.

The bird is stunned into silence, and just a few seconds later, the parrot squawks, "Stick it to him, Poopsie!"

Sign Language

A carpenter was on the third floor of a building and but he had forgotten to bring his saw up with him.

He yells down to his apprentice on the second floor but the apprentice can't hear him so the carpenter decides to use sign language.

He points to his eye (I) then his knees (need) then he moves his arms in a sawing motion (saw).

The apprentice nods, pulls down his trousers, and starts to make the motions of wanking.

The carpenter is furious, rushes down to the lad and yells, "What are you doing? I said I needed a saw."

The apprentice replies, "I know. I was just letting you know I was coming."

The Old Man

A guy is in the city when he sees an old man bawling his eyes out, so the guy asks the old timer what's the matter.

"I've had a great life," says the old man. "I was a successful carpenter, and I sold my company to a large builder for plenty of money."

The guy says, "So what's the problem?"

The old man snuffles into his sleeve and says, "I built myself a huge mansion."

The guy looks puzzled and says, "Okay, so what's the problem?"

The old man wails, "I have a beautiful car."

The guy says, "I'm with you so far, but I still don't see what the problem is."

The old man blows his nose loudly and says, "Last month I got married to a 25 year old Playboy bunny."

The guy loses his temper. "Dammit, old man – what is your problem?"

The old man sobs, "I can't remember where I live!"

Two Carpenters

Two carpenters were working on a house, an experienced guy and one new to the job. The young one, who was nailing down siding, would reach into his nail pouch, pull out a nail and either toss it over his shoulder or nail it in.

The older one asked, "Why are you wasting those perfectly good nails?"

The younger carpenter explained, "If I pull a nail out of my pouch and it's pointed toward me, I throw it away because it's defective. If it's pointed toward the house, then I nail it in."

"You idiot." the older carpenter exclaimed, "The nails pointed toward you aren't defective. They're for the other side of the house!"

Pulling Power

Carl the property developer and his carpenter buddy Pete, went bar-hopping every weekend together, and most times Carlo would go home with a woman while Pete would go home alone.

One night Pete asked Carlo his secret to picking up women.

"That's easy," said Carlo "When you're out on the dance floor and she asks you what you do for a living, don't tell her you're a carpenter. Tell her you're a lawyer."

Later Pete is dancing with a hot woman when she leans in and asks him what he does for a living.

"I'm a lawyer," says Pete.

The woman smiles and asks, "Want to go back to my place? It's just around the corner."

They go to her place, have some fun and an hour later, Pete is back in the pub telling Carlo about his success.

"I've only been a lawyer for an hour," Pete giggled, "And I've already screwed someone!"

Soft Landing

A priest, a carpenter and a soldier are in a light aircraft when they all agree to throw something out of the window.

The priest starts by throwing a bible out. Then the carpenter throws a hammer out. Then the soldier throws a grenade out.

After they throw everything out of the window and the plane has landed, the priest goes to have a look to see what happened.

He goes up to a kid that is crying and asks him what happened. He says a bible fell down and hit him.

Then the priest goes up to a man that's crying and asks what happened. The guy says a hammer just smashed his car.

The priest sees an old man laughing and asks him what happened. The old timer says he just farted and the building behind him blew up!

The Train Ride

Three carpenters and three electricians are about to board a train to a convention. As they were standing in line for tickets, the electricians noticed that the carpenters bought only one ticket between them.

The electricians bought their three tickets and boarded the train but watched the carpenters to see how they were going to manage with only one ticket.

As soon as the train left the station, the three carpenters moved from their seats and they all squeezed into one restroom.

Soon the conductor came through the carriage and knocked on the restroom door saying "Ticket please!" The door was opened slightly and an arm reached out and the one ticket was handed to the conductor.

The next day, the electricians decided to do the same thing, so they only purchased one ticket between the three of them. However they noticed the carpenters didn't purchase any tickets at all.

They all boarded the train and as soon as the train left the station, the three electricians hurry for the restroom.   A few moments later, one of the carpenters gets up from his seat, knocks on the restroom door and says, "Ticket please!"

Wedding Night Antics

The wedding date was set and three of the groom's best friends, a carpenter, an electrician and a dentist, were deciding what pranks they would play on the newly-wed couple on their wedding night.

The carpenter decided that sawing the slats off their bed would give them some laughs.

The electrician decided that wiring their bed with alternating current would be worth a giggle or two.

The dentist wouldn't reveal what he would do, but he had a sly grin and promised that his prank would be memorable.

The wedding went as planned and a few days later, each of the groom's three friends got an email which said:

I didn't mind the bed slats being sawed and the electric shock was a minor setback. But, I am going to strangle the wise guy who put the Novocaine anesthetic in the Vaseline!

Crucified

Shortly after Jesus was crucified, a young carpenter saw his opportunity to make some money from the late martyr. He began making small wooden crucifixes depicting Jesus, and people queued up to buy them.

One day, a man came in with a request saying. "I want you to make the biggest crucifix you can. I am very rich and I will pay you handsomely."

The carpenter said he would try his best and so he began. He toiled day and night, carving every intricate detail to create the biggest depiction of Jesus on the cross that he could.

When he was done, the rich man returned and upon seeing the carpenter's work, exclaimed "This is magnificent! This is the biggest carving I've ever seen!" Truly pleased, the rich man handed over the money he promised.

The carpenter accepted it, and smiled knowing he had made a huge prophet!

Reunion

A group of chippies, all aged 40, discussed where they should meet for a reunion lunch. They agreed they would meet at a place called The Bunkhouse Grill because the barmaids had big breasts and wore short-skirts.

Ten years later, at age 50, they once again discussed where they should meet for lunch.

It was agreed that they would meet at The Bunkhouse Grill because the food and service was good and there was an excellent beer selection.

Ten years later, at age 60, the chippies again discussed where they should meet for lunch.

It was agreed that they would meet at The Bunkhouse Grill because there were plenty of parking spaces, they could dine in peace and quiet, and it was good value for money.

Ten years later, at age 70, the friends discussed where they should meet for lunch.

It was agreed that they would meet at The Bunkhouse Grill because the restaurant was wheelchair accessible and had a toilet for the disabled.

Ten years later, at age 80, the retired chippies discussed where they should meet for lunch.

Finally it was agreed that they would meet at The Bunkhouse Grill because they had never been there before.

Three Daughters

A male carpenter was talking to two of his friends about their teenage daughters.

The first friend says "I was cleaning my daughter's room the other day and I found a pack of cigarettes.   I didn't even know she smoked."

The second friend says, "That's nothing. I was cleaning my daughter's room the other day and I found a half full bottle of Vodka. I didn't even know she drank."

The chippie says, "That's nothing. I was cleaning my daughter's room the other day and I found a pack of condoms. I didn't even know she had a penis."

Brown Paper Larry

A cowboy rides into a strange town and sees a carpenter doing some finishing work on a gallows so he asks, "Hey, is there going to be hanging?"

The carpenter nods. "Yep. We're fixing up the gallows so they can hang Brown Paper Larry."

The cowboy asks, "How come he's called Brown Paper Larry?"

"Well," says the carpenter, "Larry always wears clothes that are made from brown paper. Brown paper shirts. Brown paper pants. Even brown paper socks."

The cowboy contemplates this for a moment, then asks, "What are they hanging him for?"

The carpenter replies "Rustling."

On God Making Woman

And God Created Woman. He was so pleased with his creation that he calls in three of his top advisers: His chief carpenter, His chief tailor, and His chief architect. He presents his creation to them and asks for their suggestions and comments.

The carpenter said: "Too many forms, you need to straighten things out, flatten it out." God replies, "No I like it that way, but thanks."

The tailor said: "Too many strings (hair) sticking out, you need to trim them." God replies, "No I like it that way, but thanks."

The architect said: "Wonderful creation, absolutely superb, but next time, please don't place the toilets next to the reception room."

Pinocchio

Pinocchio had been getting complaints from his girlfriend. "Every time we make love," she said, "I get splinters."

So Pinocchio went back to his maker, Gipetto the carpenter, for advice.

"Sandpaper," said the carpenter. "That's what you need."

So Pinocchio took some sheets of sandpaper and went home.

A few weeks later the carpenter bumped into Pinocchio again. "How are you getting on with the girls now?" he asked.

"Who needs girls?" said Pinocchio.

Chapter 6: Carpenter Pick Up Lines

Is there anything you'd like me to screw?

I know how to use my equipment.

Want to see my tool?

I am a carpenter, I want to nail you.

I've always got wood.

I can hammer all day long.

I will show you what a real stud is.

Want to play Pinocchio? I'll sit on your face and you can tell me lies.

My tool belt really brings out the color in your eyes.

You should know that a carpenter needs a good hammer to bang in the nail.

Chapter 7: Bumper Stickers for Carpenters

Carpenter by day, deadly Ninja by night

I've got wood – permanently.

Sawdust is man glitter.

Entomologists don't bug me.

Women love me, trees fear me.

How much wood could a woodchuck chuck
If a woodchuck could chuck wood?
As much wood as a woodchuck could chuck,
If a woodchuck could chuck wood.

If a carpenter can't fix it, then no one can.

Chapter 8: Summary

Hey, that's pretty well it for this book. I hope you've enjoyed it. I've written plenty of other joke books and these are just a few sample jokes from my electricians joke book:-

Q: What do you call a Russian electrician?

A: Switchitonanov.

Q: What kind of van does an electrician drive?

A: A Volts-wagon.

Q: What is the definition of a shock absorber?

A: A careless electrician.

About the Author

Chester Croker has written many joke books and has twice been named Comedy Writer Of The Year by the International Jokers Guild.

Chester, known to his friends as Chester the Jester, worked for a while in the building trade which provided him with plenty of material for this joke book. Chester has been known to start a project with plenty of lumber and end up with what amounts to just toothpicks.

I hope you enjoyed this collection of carpentry jokes and if you did, could you please leave a review on Amazon so that other carpenters can have a good laugh too. I wood appreciate it!

If you see anything wrong, or you have a gag you would like to see included in the next version of this book, please visit the glowwormpress.com website.

Final Note:-

Let's remember that Jesus came into this world not as a philosopher or a technician, but as a carpenter.

Made in the USA
Monee, IL
13 December 2020